1st

SOAP
SOUP

SOAP SOUP

and Other Verses

by Karla Kuskin

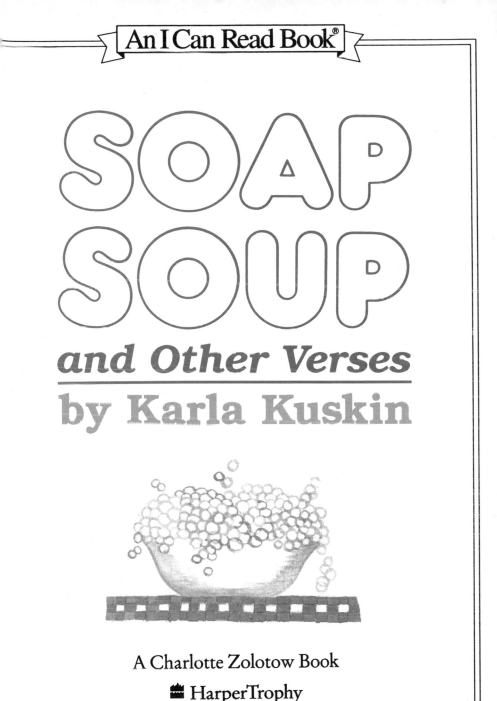

A Charlotte Zolotow Book

HarperTrophy

A Division of HarperCollins*Publishers*

Soap Soup and Other Verses
Copyright © 1992 by Karla Kuskin
Printed in the U.S.A. All rights reserved.

Library of Congress Cataloging-in-Publication Data
Kuskin, Karla.
    Soap soup and other verses / by Karla Kuskin.
        p.   cm. —(An I can read book)
    "A Charlotte Zolotow book."
    Summary: A collection of poems about discovering the world.
    ISBN 0-06-023571-3. — ISBN 0-06-023572-1 (lib. bdg.)
    ISBN 0-06-444174-1 (pbk.)
    1. Children's poetry, American.   [1. American poetry.]
I. Title.   II. Series.
PS3561.U79S58   1992   91-22947
811'.54—dc20   CIP
                                                      AC

First Harper Trophy edition, 1994.

For Mary and her husband

Cloud and sky.

Wet and dry.

Wind and weather.

6

Ice and cream.

Sleep and dream.

Some words seem

to go together.

Soft and skin.

Nose and chin.

Some words fit right in

together.

The outside me

(the me you see)

begins with skin.

And there

above my chin

beneath my hair:

one mouth

a nose

two eyes

and ears

that let the outside in.

My head is here.

My hat is there.

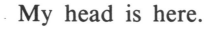

My head sits underneath

my hair.

My hair sits underneath

my hat.

And that is why

my hair lies flat.

10

This is the way a mouth goes.

Up: smile.

Down: frown.

Bottom lip stuck out:

pout.

If my eyes

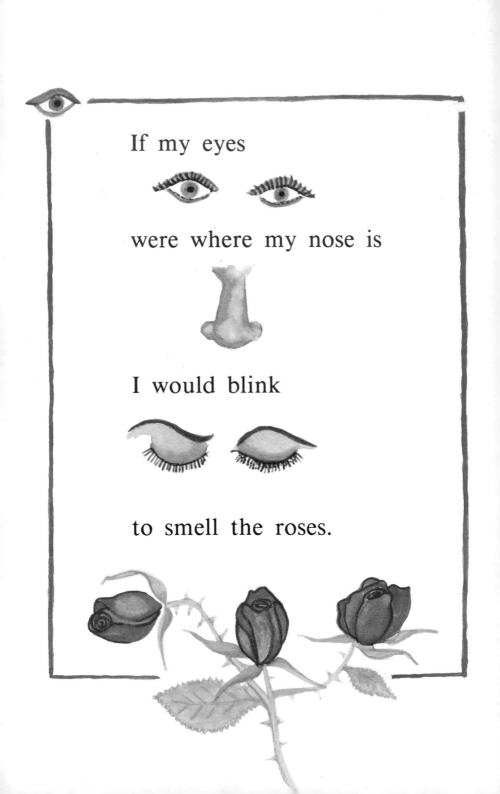

were where my nose is

I would blink

to smell the roses.

Isn't it queer

that an ear

can hear?

Arms bend at the elbows

when you are lifting up

a fork

a spoon

a baseball bat

a cup

a pup

a cat

or if you stop

to tip your hat.

These are my knees.

My knees are bony places

that bend when I am walking

down the block

or running races.

16

This is my foot.

My foot is mine

and that is true.

I know because

my foot is in my shoe.

Or does that foot belong to you?

Then what is it doing in my shoe?

I am standing on the sand.

All my toes are here.

I can see each one because

the water is so clear.

Let us walk across the sand

foot by foot

hand by hand

hand by foot

foot by hand.

Let us walk across the sand.

Cats and dogs

it is hot out.

Rats and mice

it is hot.

Sun and stars

and Earth and Mars

It is five, four, three,

too hot!

Chocolate

vanilla

coffee

and peach.

Let me have a cone of each.

When I am through

I will have some more.

Then I will fall down on the floor.

Put the dinner

on the table.

Then sit down

and eat it, Mabel.

And if you are able,

Mabel,

you may also eat

the table.

To eat an egg

and eat it right

first of all you eat the white.

Then you eat the yellow yolk.

Then you take your spoon

and poke

the awful slipping, dripping stuff.

And then you yell,

"I have had enough."

Butter

butter

butter

butter

that is a word

I love to utter.

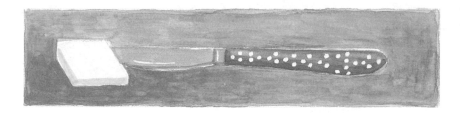

Thin or fat,

fat or thin.

Open your mouth

and the food goes in.

And what you eat—

a bit of sweet,

a bite of stew—

each bite and bit

turns into you.

I have a hunch

I won't like lunch.

And

if I do not eat my dinner

I will get a little thinner.

I am making stew for you.

First I will put in a shoe.

Then I will put in some glue.

Then some dust

from off the floor.

Would you like a little more?

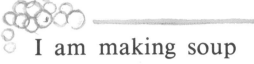

I am making soup

of soap.

James will drink it up

I hope.

I have not been friends with James

since he called me all those names.

To the Person I Am Mad at Today

You know what I like to do?

Make terrible faces at you.

I am very fond of you

but

I get tired of you too.

There is nothing more boring
than watching someone snoring.

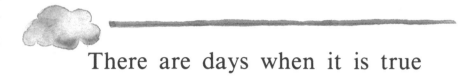

There are days when it is true

nothing

nothing

pleases you.

When people cough

and cough

and cough

I wish someone

would turn them off.

When you open your mouth

the snow snows in.

The flakes are fat

and flat and thin

and some of them land

on your nose

and chin.

It is snowing

and snowing

so what shall we eat?

The snow looks so good

I will make you a treat.

I am a very fine cook

and I have what it takes.

Come into the kitchen.

I am baking some flakes.

The tree has leaves

and I have hair.

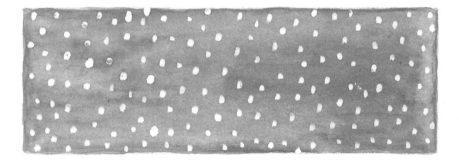

In winter

when the tree is bare,

I wear a hat

to warm my head

and keep my ears

from turning red.

39

In winter there is too much ice.

In summer

ice is very nice.

I am sick of boots

and winter clothes.

I want to wear

just shorts and toes.

Look out of the window.

Listen to the wind blow.

Outside in

and inside out,

listen to the wild wind shout.

Summer is gone

and so are the roses.

Sidewalks are icy

and so are our noses.

Noses are rosy

and so are our cheeks

and will be for many long

wintery weeks.

Out to walk,

dog and I

raced the clouds,

44

saw the sky

blowing by,

gray with rain.

Dog and I

raced home again.

Dog and I

met some birds.

Dog barked,

birds chirped,

I spoke words.

Birds flew,

dog ran,

I walked home,

ate a cookie,

wrote a poem.

This is the baby.

Count his toes,

count his fingers,

and count his nose.

This is the baby's tabby cat.

These are her paws.

This is her hat.

These are her socks,

her shoes,

her gloves.

This is the cat

the baby loves.

Grandma is old

and I am young

and when we stroll

through clover

a lot of funny songs are sung,

a lot of talk talked over.

Tick goes the clock.

The clock goes tock.

I like to sit

and watch you knit

a hat or sock

and hear the knitting needles

click

tock, tick.

52

The sun is warm,

the wool is blue.

One sock is done

tick, click,

tock, clock.

The sock is woolly, warm

and blue.

I wonder when there will be two.

If you must,

dust.

Dust the lamp

and dust the chair,

but do not dust me—

I am sitting there.

I have listened,

listened for a long time.

I have listened to you

as I did before.

I have sat and listened,

listened for a long time.

I refuse to listen

to you anymore.

There is a me inside of me,

inside

the outside me

you see.

I am beside myself

with glee.

I ho

and ho

and hee

and hee,

58

I hee

and hee

and ho

and ho.

I wonder why

I'm ho-ing so.

Dreams are life you live asleep.

But then you wake

and stretch

and yawn

and look around.

The dreams are gone.

There is a bed

inside my head

and when the day is long

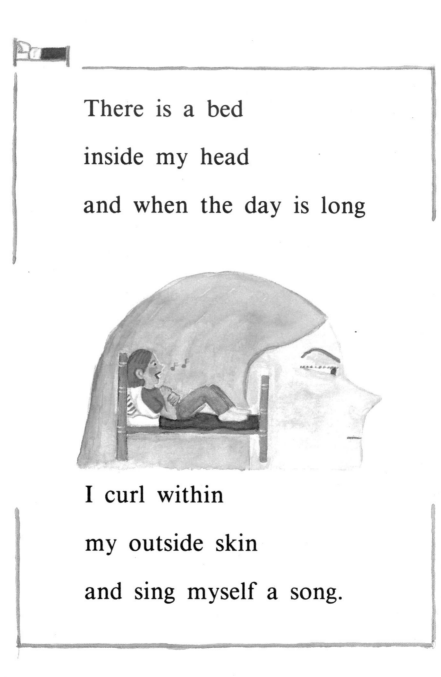

I curl within

my outside skin

and sing myself a song.

Where we are

is very far

from every star.

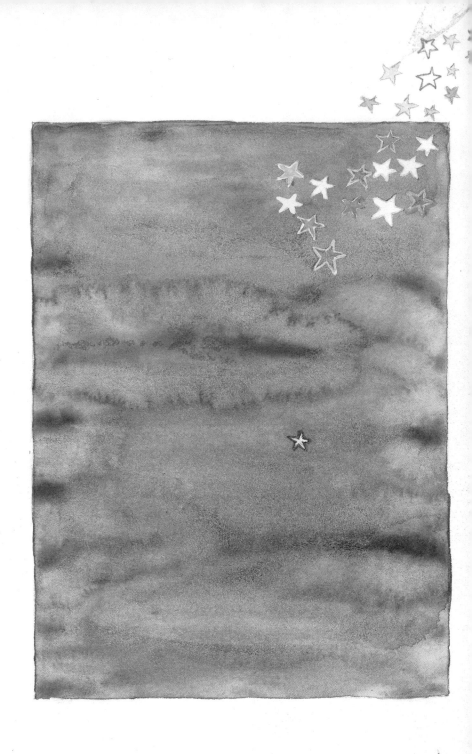